BECOMING HOME

FRAMES
BARNA GROUP

BECOMING HOME

Adoption, Foster Care, and Mentoring—Living Out
God's Heart for Orphans

JEDD MEDEFIND

RE/FRAMES BY FRANCIS CHAN,
JIM DALY, RUSLAN MALIUTA, DAVID PLATT,
AND CARISSA WOODWYK

ZONDERVAN®

CONTENTS

....

WHY YOU NEED FRAMES

These days, you probably find yourself with less time than ever.

Everything seems like it's moving at a faster pace — except your ability to keep up.

Somehow, you are weighed down with more obligations than you have ever had before.

Life feels more complicated. More complex.

If you're like most people, you probably have lots of questions about how to live a life that matters. You feel as though you have more to learn than can possibly be learned. But with smaller chunks of time and more sources of information than ever before, where can you turn for real insight and livable wisdom?

Barna Group has produced this series to examine the complicated issues of life and to help you live more meaningfully. We call it FRAMES — like a good set of eyeglasses that help you see the world more clearly ... or a work of art perfectly hung that invites you to look more closely ... or a building's skeleton, the part that is most essential to its structure.

The FRAMES Season 1 collection provides thoughtful and concise, data-driven and visually appealing insights for anyone who wants a more faith-driven and fulfilling life. In each FRAME we couple new cultural analysis from our team at Barna with an essay from leading voices in the field, providing information and ideas for you to digest in a more easily consumed number of words.

After all, it's a fast-paced world, full of words and images vying for your attention. Most of us have a number of half-read or "read someday" books on our shelves. But each FRAME aims to give you the essential information and real-life application behind one of today's most crucial trends in less than one-quarter the length of most books. These are big ideas in small books— designed so you truly can read less but know more. And the infographics and ideas in this FRAME are intended for share-ability. So read it, then find someone to "frame" with these ideas, and keep the conversation going (see "Share This Frame" on page 88).

Furthermore, each FRAME brings a distinctly Christian point of view to today's trends. In times of uncertainty, people look for guides. And we believe the Christian community is trying to make sense of the dramatic social changes happening around us.

Over the past thirty years, Barna Group has built a reputation as a trusted analyst of religion and culture. We offer cultural discernment for the Christian community by thoughtful analysts who care enough to tell the truth about what's really happening in today's society.

So sit back, but not for long. With FRAMES we invite you to read less and know more.

DAVID KINNAMAN
FRAMES, executive producer
president / Barna Group

ROXANNE STONE
FRAMES, general editor
vice president / Barna Group

Learn more at www.barnaframes.com.

FRAMES

TITLE	20 and Something	Becoming Home	Fighting for Peace	Greater Expectations
PURPOSE	Have the Time of Your Life (And Figure It All Out Too)	Adoption, Foster Care, and Mentoring – Living Out God's Heart for Orphans	Your Role in a Culture Too Comfortable with Violence	Succeed (and Stay Sane) in an On-Demand, All-Access, Always-On Age
AUTHOR	David H. Kim	Jedd Medefind	Carol Howard Merritt & Tyler Wigg-Stevenson	Claire Diaz-Ortiz
KEY TREND	27% of young adults have clear goals for the next 5 years	62% of Americans believe Christians have a responsibility to adopt	47% of adults say they're less comfortable with violence than 10 years ago	42% of people are unhappy with their work/life balance

PERFECT FOR SMALL GROUP DISCUSSION

FRAMES Season 1: DVD
FRAMES Season 1: The Complete
                    Collection

READ LESS.
KNOW MORE.

The Hyperlinked Life	Multi-Careering	Sacred Roots	Schools in Crisis	Wonder Women
Live with Wisdom in an Age of Information Overload	Do Work That Matters at Every Stage of Your Journey	Why the Church Still Matters	They Need Your Help (Whether You Have Kids or Not)	Navigating the Challenges of Motherhood, Career, and Identity
Jun Young & David Kinnaman	Bob Goff	Jon Tyson	Nicole Baker Fulgham	Kate Harris
71% of adults admit they're overwhelmed by information	75% of adults are looking for ways to live a more meaningful life	51% of people don't think it's important to attend church	46% of Americans say public schools are worse than 5 years ago	72% of women say they're stressed

#BarnaFrames

www.barnaframes.com

BEFORE YOU READ

- When you hear "loving orphans," what comes to mind?

- Have you ever considered adoption or foster care? What were some of the factors that went into your decision whether or not to follow through with it?

- Why do you think Scripture places a particular emphasis on God's love for the orphan?

- Even if your family didn't adopt or foster a child, what are other ways you imagine you could care for orphans?

- When have you seen adoption or orphan care go wrong? What are some fears or negative perceptions you have about it?

- How does your church support orphan care—through services, support for adoptive or fostering families, or in other ways?

- What has caused you to be interested in this topic and this book? What has God placed in your heart that draws you to adoption, fostering, or orphan care?

BECOMING HOME

Adoption, Foster Care, and Mentoring—Living Out
God's Heart for Orphans

INFOGRAPHICS

Who is **ADOPTING?**

While adopting and fostering remain rare, practicing Christians are more than twice as likely as the general population to adopt and significantly more likely to consider adoption or fostering.

5% 38% 3% 31%

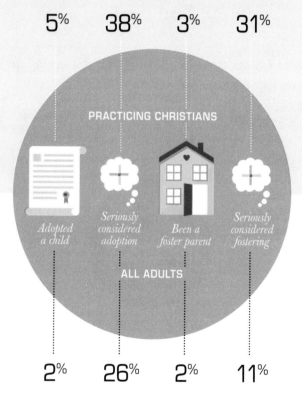

PRACTICING CHRISTIANS

Adopted a child *Seriously considered adoption* *Been a foster parent* *Seriously considered fostering*

ALL ADULTS

2% 26% 2% 11%

"Christians are more than twice as likely to have adopted a child"

*Among adults under the age of 50

WHILE NEARLY TWO IN FIVE PRACTICING CHRISTIANS HAVE CONSIDERED ADOPTION, ONLY 5% HAVE ACTUALLY DONE IT

*What keeps people from adopting?**

- Never thought about it: **28%**
- It's too expensive: **25%**
- No desire: **23%**
- Prefer to have biological children: **23%**
- My spouse doesn't want to: **14%**
- The process is too intimidating: **11%**
- Don't know where to start: **9%**
- Too many risks: **9%**
- Too much paperwork: **9%**
- It takes too long: **8%**
- I have my own kids: **8%**

*Totals equal more than 100% as respondents could choose more than one answer

In the next 5 years, how likely are you to …

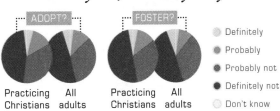

ADOPT?
Practicing Christians   All adults

FOSTER?
Practicing Christians   All adults

- Definitely
- Probably
- Probably not
- Definitely not
- Don't know

ORPHAN CARE:
A special mandate for Christians

Most people – whether believers or not – would say
Christians have a special responsibility to care for the orphan.
However, most active churchgoers say their church
offers little help to adoptive families – or if their church does
offer help, they don't know about it.

*73% of Americans believe it's
a positive thing for Christians to focus
on adoption and foster care*

62% of all adults
believe Christians
have a responsibility
to adopt

77% of practicing
Christians believe
Christians have a
responsibility to adopt

"My church makes a special effort to encourage adoption or foster care"*

*among practicing Christians under age 50

30% YES **59%** NO **11%** I DON'T KNOW

"My church helps with …"

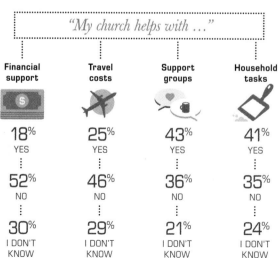

Financial support	Travel costs	Support groups	Household tasks
18% YES	25% YES	43% YES	41% YES
52% NO	46% NO	36% NO	35% NO
30% I DON'T KNOW	29% I DON'T KNOW	21% I DON'T KNOW	24% I DON'T KNOW

BECOMING HOME

Adoption, Foster Care, and Mentoring—Living Out
God's Heart for Orphans

FRAMEWORK

BY BARNA GROUP

Adoption, foster care and other ways of aiding vulnerable children represent vital engagement with a critical social justice need. But they also offer a rich theological expression of our relationship with God. So it only makes sense that Christians would be the first to champion the cause of orphans around the globe.

Our FRAMES research shows Christians, in fact, are deeply engaged in this issue. If you're reading this book, you are probably one of those people who are making a difference. Maybe you're an adoptive or foster parent, or a mentor yourself. Or maybe you'd like to be, and you're doing the research, praying through the process, and getting increasingly excited about the possibility of inviting a child into your home. Or maybe you support organizations working to serve orphans around the world. Or maybe you're not personally called to or able to adopt, but all the same, you've caught on to the passion of God's heart for orphans, and you want to help. But for such a great need as this, how does one get started?

That's what this book is designed to help you find out.

Adoption by the Numbers

If the legal record is any indication, America has come a long way in the past few decades in orphan care. Only a trickle of seven pieces of federal legislation passed concerning child protection, welfare, and adoption between 1974's Child Abuse Prevention and Treatment Act (CAPTA) and the Family Preservation and Support

Services Program Act of 1993. Over the next two decades, however, almost three times as many bills were signed into law.

Still, the orphan care and adoption movement is in its infancy. The FRAMES research shows just 2% of US adults under the age of 50 have adopted or ever been a foster parent. Only a quarter (26%) have given serious thought to adopting a child, and less than two in ten (17%) say they are probably or definitely willing to adopt a child in the next five years. About the same say they have seriously thought of being a foster parent (21%) or are likely to foster a child (11%) in the same time frame.

Though many countries don't keep reliable adoption records, the UN reports there are approximately 260,000 domestic and international adoptions a year. The United States, with more than 127,000 adoptions per year, accounts for nearly half of the total number of adoptions worldwide.[1] Meaning a mere 2% of the American population is carrying a huge weight of the global responsibility for adopting children without parents. This fact alone highlights two things. First, that America is leading the way in adoption. Second, that there is far more work to be done. And since over half of Americans (54%) say they would rather adopt from their own country—and 78% of parents who have adopted did so within the United States—this leaves a gaping need for adoptive parents of children in other countries.

The FRAMES research found that while the gender split of adopted children in the US is about half and

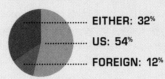

78% of adoptive parents adopted from within the US

And most people considering adoption prefer to adopt domestically

EITHER: 32%

US: 54%

FOREIGN: 12%

half, this changes when it comes to international adoptions. Two-thirds of children adopted internationally (67%) are female. Most of these families adopt one child (75%), fewer adopt two (23%), and very rarely do they adopt more than two (3%). When it comes to having biological children as well as adopted children, adoptive parents are split: About half (48%) of adoptive parents have no biological children of their own, 43% had biological kids before adopting, and 9% had biological kids after adopting.

While the majority of adoptive parents are non-Hispanic white (73%), non-Hispanic white adopted children are actually the minority (37%). The majority of child adoptions, then, result in multi-ethnic families. While raising a child of a different culture or ethnicity might be perceived as a hurdle to some, the FRAMES data show most adoptive parents don't see it this way. An overwhelming 93% of Americans say they support multi-ethnic adoption. About one-third say they support it when the family is willing to make changes so the child will appreciate their ethnic background.

Parents have more reservations about adopting children with various risk factors such as special needs, health problems, or behavioral issues. Such reservations are notable since 39% of children available for adoption have special health care needs, and a quarter of them (26%) have moderate to severe health problems.[2] Even among healthy children, there are risk factors for older children looking for adoptive parents. Only half of prospective parents say they are open to adopting older children, who, they perceive, might bring troubled pasts and/ or greater behavioral issues into the home, more so than infants.

Family Portrait

Among families who have adopted, the majority adopted one child. Families may or may not also have biological children.

How many kids have you adopted?

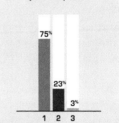

75%

23%

3%

1 2 3

No biological kids: **48%**

Biological kid(s) before adopting: **43%**

Biological kid(s) only after adopting: **9%**

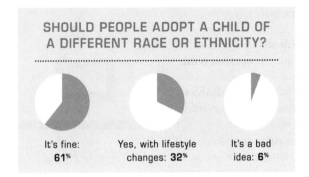

SHOULD PEOPLE ADOPT A CHILD OF
A DIFFERENT RACE OR ETHNICITY?

It's fine:
61%

Yes, with lifestyle
changes: **32%**

It's a bad
idea: **6%**

The Christian Adoption Movement

Today, practicing Christians are the most likely to
adopt—5% have done so, compared to 2% of all
Americans. They are also more likely, though only
slightly, to be foster parents (3% compared to 2% of all
Americans). Additionally, about one-third of practicing
Christians (30%) say their church makes adoption an
intentional priority.

The FRAMES research finds that more than three-
quarters of practicing Christians (77%) believe Christians have at least "some" responsibility to adopt. This
sentiment is echoed by the general population, 62%
of whom agree Christians have a responsibility to
adopt. Additionally, about three-quarters of Americans
(73%) say it's a positive thing for Christians to focus on
adoption and foster care.

But Are the Kids All Right?

For all the complications of the adoption process, the ultimate question is this: What is best for the child?

Half of the FRAMES survey respondents (49%) feel a child should be raised by whoever can provide the best care for them, even if it is not their biological parents. In comparison, 40% believe a child should be removed from their biological parents only if there is immediate danger. Very few unequivocally believe children should always be raised by biological parents—only 5% say children should stay with their biological parents even if it's an abusive home.

Regardless of these varying opinions, the data show adopted children fare just as well, or even better, when compared to the national average. Adopted children are less likely to live in poverty, for example. Just one in ten (12%) live in households below the poverty threshold—compared to 18% of children in the general population. Furthermore, more than two-thirds of adopted kids (69%) live with two married parents, and a large majority of parents (81%) report having a warm and close relationship with their adopted child. Adoptive parents are also more likely to read to their children every day (68% compared to 48%), sing or tell stories every day (73% compared to 59%), and encourage their children to participate in extracurricular activities (85% compared to 81%).

Conclusion

More than any other community, practicing Christians have engaged adoption and foster care. It's an encouraging prospect, and yet there is much unfinished work. For example, in 2012 alone, 399,546 children were in the public foster care system in the United States; of those eligible for adoption 52,000 were adopted while 102,000 were left waiting at the end of the year.[3] And in the rest of the world, untold thousands are without a safe family environment in which to thrive.

It's an incredible social need, one which the church is uniquely poised to engage. However, first Christians must be prepared and equipped to help without hurting. Jedd Medefind, the president of the Christian Alliance for Orphans (CAFO) and an adoptive parent himself, writes this FRAME to do just that. You'll also hear from Francis Chan, Carissa Woodwyk, Ruslan Maliuta, David Platt, and Jim Daly as they share their own stories and experiences with the orphan care movement.

Whether you are an adoptive parent already, considering foster care or adoption, or simply interested in learning more, this FRAME is here to give you a starting point for your next step. ◆

BECOMING HOME

Adoption, Foster Care, and Mentoring—Living Out God's Heart for Orphans

THE FRAME

BY JEDD MEDEFIND

I'll never forget that phone call.

It came at one of the happiest times of our lives, just weeks before my wife, Rachel, and I were supposed to leave for Ethiopia to bring our adopted daughter home. But when a heart opens to an orphaned child, both joy and ache often enter together.

The voice on the other end was tight, stilted. It was a staff member at our adoption agency, someone who'd become a good friend. "Jedd, we have something difficult to tell you ... about your daughter." A long pause. "Can you get home soon, to be with Rachel and then call back?"

As I hung up, I felt a sudden, suffocating need for air. More than a year previously, Rachel and I had decided to adopt. Like most couples considering adoption, the process had included months of prayer and deliberation. Can we afford it? How would this affect our biological daughters, then three and one year old? What would be different about parenting a child of another race?

But amid the questions, the final choice became clear. We knew we wanted to grow our family. And while we could do that with less cost and complexity via natural birth, we knew countless kids out there needed families. Why not bring one into ours?

I know many things now I wish I'd known back then. Things about adoption ethics, what wounded children need to heal, and how much diversity there is within the vast lumped-together group we call "orphans."

These are things I want you to know now—a primary reason I'm writing for this book. But I think we did have the main concerns right: Children need families. Millions are growing up without one. God has a special concern for these kids. And we should too.

Long before Rachel and I married, I spent my first year out of college with three close friends, traveling and volunteering in several developing countries. In every place, from Guatemala to Russia to southern Africa, the plight of the many orphans we met weighed heavily on me. When I returned to the US, their stories helped give me a new focus, spurring me to give up a spot at law school for a path I hoped would enable more impact on the world than the constraints of a big law firm.

Years passed, but the memories still tugged at me: Street children in Guatemala who had leaped onto cars in traffic to wash windshields, hoping for a small recompense. The teen boys I wrestled with in a Russian orphanage—their bravado barely masking the childlike craving for affirmation underneath. A blind toddler in India, who sank her fingernails into the back of my neck as I tried to set her back in her crib.

In light of the world's vast hurt, Rachel and I knew a single adoption was like shooting a squirt gun at a building fire. But we also saw it could change things for one child, and we suspected it would change us too. We wanted to make God's grace tangible in a hurting world, not only at work and ministry but also in our family. Adoption struck us as just one more choice along that path.

After mountains of paperwork and endless waiting, we were matched with a little girl in Ethiopia. Our friends and relatives rejoiced with us. At seven months old, she weighed six pounds and seven ounces. We pored over the pictures of her emaciated frame and wide, deep eyes. We loved her immediately. Her name would be Ayana Rachel Medefind. We prayed for her daily, yearned to begin nursing her toward health. Pictures of Ayana graced our mantel, and the workers at her children's home hung a snapshot of our family on the pink-painted box that served as her crib. She was ours.

Then that phone call from our adoption agency came. When I arrived home, Rachel and I called the agency back, our hearts pounding. The words we heard were the ones we'd feared the most. "We're so, so sad to tell you this ... Ayana came down with pneumonia yesterday. They took her to the doctor, but her little body didn't have the strength ... we're so sorry."

It's amazing how much you can love a child you've never held, how you mourn when she's lost to this earthly life forever. We grieved deeply. Yet we knew our pain was one small sip of the world's deep pain. So many parents have lost their children; oceans of children have lost their parents. It also drove home a simple truth, one we've seen countless times since: Every decision to love an orphan brings beauty and sorrow intertwined.

This is true not only for adoptive parents but for others involved in orphan care as well. Both celebration and sadness come with mentoring a foster youth, or babysitting an adopted child with special needs, or investing deeply in efforts to care for widows and their children. Opening ourselves to the orphan exposes our hearts to the world at its most deeply broken parts ... and both joy and heartache are sure to follow.

Six months after Ayana died, Rachel and I did finally travel to Ethiopia. We would soon rejoice to meet the girl who would become our daughter, Eden. But first we desired to visit Ayana's grave.

A worker from the children's home guided us through the weeds and ramshackle markers of the graveyard, then withdrew to give us privacy. Rachel and I knelt on the dusty ground, tears rolling down both of our faces. "Want to sing?" she whispered. My voice choked as I breathed the words to "Be Still My Soul." But something much like joy came spilling up too. I never got to hold that little girl who now lay beneath the cracked earth. I never stroked her head or sang her a lullaby. But she had been loved, deeply. Not only by us, but by the grandparents, aunts, uncles, and so many friends who'd adopted her too. In her short span, she had touched lives across the world.

I believe I'll see Ayana someday. When I do, I hope I'll get to sing her that lullaby. Or maybe she'll sing one to me.

This matchless beauty, this unspeakable pain — all woven together — this is at the root of God's love for the orphan. It is his invitation to each of us as well.

THE MODERN CRISIS

The reality of orphans, of course, is nothing new. Some of the earliest words of Scripture, written thousands of years ago, address this need directly.

What is new in our day is the vast scale of the need. Global diseases like AIDS, famine, extreme poverty, and war have stolen millions of parents from their children. At the same time, these scourges have debilitated the capacity of extended family to take in orphaned children.

As a widow in Kenya observed, "In the past, people used to care for the orphans and love them, but these days there are so many, and many people have died who could have assisted them, and therefore orphanhood is a common phenomenon, not strange. The few who are alive cannot support them."[4]

Latest estimates project that more than 150 million children worldwide meet the definition of orphan, with at least one parent dead. Nearly 18 million "double orphans" have lost both parents. It's a staggering figure, one that's difficult to fathom. But imagine it like this: That is more than enough children to fill 180 Super Bowl stadiums.[5]

Beyond the numbers are very real situations of individual children, which vary tremendously. Some double orphans are taken in by caring neighbors; others face a brutal existence on the streets. Some "single orphans" thrive with their one surviving parent; many others face severe deprivation along with their widowed mother. In still other cases, both of a child's parents may be alive, yet their neglect, abandonment, or abuse resulted in virtual orphanhood for the child.

Each situation is unique and complex. But we can be sure of one thing: Orphans are the most vulnerable people on our planet.

This vulnerability touches every aspect of an orphan's life. Both single and double orphans are much more likely than other children to be malnourished and stunted in growth.[6] Even when living with a surviving parent or relative, orphans are less likely to attend school and more likely to fall behind and drop out.[7] Orphans often lack funds for basic medical treatment, food, and school supplies.

Then there's the risk posed to orphans by those who know their unique vulnerability—and exploit it. A 2002 assessment in Ethiopia found that more than three-quarters of child domestic workers were orphans. Of the child domestics interviewed, 80% did not have the right to quit their job. They worked over eleven hours per day with no days off. Most were not allowed to play with their employers' children, listen to the radio, or watch TV. More than a third weren't provided with any schooling.[8]

Perhaps most disturbing is the way human traffickers victimize orphans. A study in Moldova found that children growing up in institutions are ten times more vulnerable to trafficking than other children.[9] A 2002 assessment in Zambia found that of all children engaged in prostitution, almost half were double orphans, and another quarter were single orphans. Their average age was fifteen. Their typical daily earnings varied from sixty-three cents to $7. The majority, particularly younger children, rarely made as much as $2 a day. These children were forced to service three to four clients on an average day.[10] The head of a street children ministry in Brazil put it to me this way: "We have to assume every girl coming to us has been trafficked."

This tragic reality doesn't lurk only in far-off places, either. The head of Florida's trafficking task force estimates that 70% of child trafficking victims are foster youth.[11] A study in New York found that 75% of children who were commercially exploited for sex had spent time in foster care.[12]

Today, there are roughly 400,000 children in foster care in the US at any given time. They have been removed from their families not as a result of any fault of their own but because those who should have cared for them didn't or couldn't. About 100,000 have become wards of the state and now wait for adoption into a family.[13] For the rest, the goal is to be reunified with their family someday. But they live today in great need of caring foster homes, mentors, advocates, and friends.

From Lusaka to Los Angeles, all of these are the children the Bible repeatedly calls God's people to care for and protect. They face the world without the full protection, provision, and nurture a father and mother uniquely provide. These are children God loves deeply. The prophet Isaiah put it succinctly: "Take up the cause of the fatherless" (Isaiah 1:17, NIV84).

A Job We Can't Outsource

Much of my professional career has been in government, from the California legislature to the White House. It's deeply rewarding to contribute to public policy that can make a difference for hurting people, from the Mentoring Children of Prisoners program and the Adoption Tax Credit to the President's Emergency Plan for AIDS Relief (PEPFAR).

Yes, I've observed that government can often create new problems even as it tries to solve old ones. But I've also seen firsthand that government can—and must—play a vital role for vulnerable children. Healthy justice systems protect children from abuse and exploitation. Government can also help marshal physical goods like disaster relief or medicine on an enormous scale.

But as vital as these things are, government alone can never meet the deepest needs of a child. As a veteran of Colorado's child welfare system once said to me, "Government makes a terrible parent." The things that matter most—love, nurture, and belonging—can only be provided person to person as individuals and families care for each precious child.

James 1:27 says, "Religion that God our Father accepts as pure and faultless is this: to look after orphans and widows in their distress and to keep oneself from being polluted by the world." This is a high charge. And it is something governments cannot do. That's why the church cannot outsource James 1:27 to government or NGOs. As Christians, as people God has expressly called to love the orphan, we have an irreplaceable role to fill.

A Call to Each of Us

As we'll explore throughout this book, caring for orphans is an undertaking for the entire church community to engage together. Not every Christian is called to foster or adopt. But every Christian community is called to embody the pure religion that includes caring for orphans and widows in their distress. No other institution in the world is capable of embracing orphans and supporting their families like the local church. This is something we can only do together—becoming home for those who most need it.

And each of us can play a part.

For Andrew Schneidler, a lawyer in Seattle, that began with offering low- and no-cost legal help to families adopting from foster care. Not long ago, he left his law firm to create the Permanence Project, housed in his local church, to provide these services on a larger scale. Andrew hopes to find volunteer lawyers in every state to do the same.[14]

For Nickolay Rykov, who was adopted from an orphanage by a Ukrainian family, this includes riding his bike across Ukraine with other former orphans, urging families to consider adoption. Nickolay's hope is as simple as it is monumental: "That every child would have a family."[15]

Christians at Plant Sciences, Inc., in California have harnessed their agriculture expertise for orphans and widows worldwide. Partnering with an excellent global orphan care ministry, PSI is helping create highly successful strawberry farms in Africa, Eastern Europe, and Central America. The farms help fund schools for vulnerable children, while also providing good jobs for widows and other caregivers of orphans.[16]

Whether student or stay-at-home mom, restaurateur or retiree, we all have a role to play in the church *becoming home* for children who need it most.

More Than a Mandate

JT and Sara Olson already had four children when they sensed God nudging them toward adoption. Both excited and daunted, they decided to move forward. The year ahead was heavy with paperwork, prayer, financial sacrifice … and waiting. Finally, they found themselves at the orphanage in China where little Grace lived, ready to take her home for good.

Their journey, however, was just beginning. Like many children who've known little touch or affection, Grace had major developmental delays. Though eighteen months old, she still couldn't roll over or form a word. She had scars where she'd been tied to her crib. Grace greeted Sara and JT by screaming nonstop for hours.

Confident that love would overcome the challenges, JT and Sara returned home upbeat. But over the next few weeks it became clear Grace's wounds were deep. Fear seemed to grip her. When asleep, she would bolt upright at the slightest sound, then remain awake for hours. She seemed incapable of laughter. Worst of all, Grace rejected any hint of intimacy. If her parents held her too close or put their cheek against her skin, she would cry with such ferocity that her capillaries ruptured, leaving what looked like a rash all over her body.

At their lowest moments, both JT and Sara wondered, "What have we done to our family? Will we ever be normal again?"

What carried them through the darkness was the same thing that had motivated them to adopt in the first place. They were responding to what they knew of God's heart and what he'd done for them.

"God adopted us at profound cost to himself," JT explains. "So adopting an orphan, even when very difficult, is just a small retelling of the gospel. That story too includes suffering."

A Mirror of God's Heart

There is no doubt the Bible carries a clear mandate to care for orphans. But caring for orphans is not mandate alone. It is foremost a mirror of God's heart.

Long before Isaiah exhorted the Jews to "take up the cause of the fatherless," the Torah described God's character in almost the very same language: "He defends the cause of the fatherless."[17] The prophet Hosea told Israel to say to God, "In you the fatherless find compassion."[18] The Psalms express, "A father to the fatherless, a defender of widows, is God in his holy dwelling. God sets the lonely in families."[19]

What a contrast to the gods of Greece and Rome! They
set their eyes on athletes, generals, and kings. Zeus
and Artemis and Hermes sought out the beautiful and
sleek and powerful. But the God of the Bible places his
special attention on the most vulnerable and destitute:
the orphaned child.

Most breathtaking of all, this is not only the orphan's
story. It is ours as well. For the heart of the Christian
story—the gospel—is how God sought us when we
were destitute and alone. How he invites us to live as his
daughters and sons.[20]

It is this matchless narrative that animates the Christian to care for orphans, to love as he first loved us.
Any other motivators like duty, guilt, and idealism can
indeed move us. But they will not carry us the distance
when the going gets tough. And if we choose to open
our hearts and lives to the orphan—whether via
adoption, fostering, mentoring, or otherwise—it will
get tough.

Here is the hard truth: Every orphan's journey begins
with a tragedy. Often, it gets worse from there. This is
true for the orphan of AIDS or abandonment or civil
war, as well as children in the US foster care system.
They have tasted the world at its most broken. And as
we draw near to them, we will taste some of that pain as
well. Sometimes as inconvenience. Sometimes as lack of
comfort. Sometimes in downright anguish.

Like JT and Sara, we may struggle to bring healing to
a wounded child. We may see the boy we've mentored
return to gang life or the girl we're fostering steal from

our desk. It may seem that for every child we lift from the streets, ten take their place. We may experience rejection from the very children to whom we've given our hearts—just as our heavenly Father often does. So if we are to go the distance, we must drink from a deeper source than guilt, duty, or idealism alone. We must draw from the wellspring of God's fathomless love.

It took a year before JT and Sara began to notice Grace laugh often or smile readily. The sacrifices and tears preceding that milestone were innumerable, and many more were to follow. But bit by bit, small change by small change, Grace responded to her parents' love—just as they sought to love her in response to how God loves them.

Years later, Sara told me, "Grace is the snuggliest thing, the most tender, compassionate girl you can imagine. She brings so much joy to our family, to each and every person. We are all just crazy about her. It seems nearly every day when JT looks at Grace, sees a picture of her, or retells a story about something she has done, he remarks, 'I am a rich man!' "

JT and Sara went on to launch the Both Hands Foundation, which supports both international adoptions and in-country orphan care, while also repairing the homes of widows in the US.[21] They have drunk deeply of what it means to become home for a child who needed it ... and now are helping many others do the same.

Looking back, Sara said, "If we'd adopted just for ourselves or only to rescue an orphan, I'm not sure we would have made it through. But we knew from the start that Christ had walked the kind of path we were taking long before we did. Our giving was just a reflection of his, and we knew his love would surround us—even if the outcome turned out to be not what we'd hoped. That kept us there, even in the most desperate moments."

Love has overcome, though not without great cost. This story is retold in many an adoption, and in countless other expressions of care for orphans. Most of all, it is a humble echo of the story of the gospel.

An Ancient Commitment

It's a kind of love that goes back to the earliest days of the church.

In ancient Rome, infants were often abandoned on the outskirts of cities. The practice was called exposing. Whether a child was unwanted because it was the wrong gender or malformed or simply inconvenient, it was taken outside the city walls and left alone. The sun, rain, or wild animals did the rest of the work.

But Christians, who were often a persecuted minority at the time, made a practice of going outside the city walls, finding these children, and bringing them home, sometimes even raising them as their own. [22]

Throughout history, Christians at their best have reflected the same commitment. Candidates for leadership in the early church were to be "lovers of orphans,"[23] and this heart has always been visible in healthy Christian communities.

From the outset, this movement has included diverse expressions of care. It spans foster care and mentoring, adoption, support of global orphan care, and much more. All of this reflects a Christian commitment that is both ancient and renewed.

Adoption

Adoption is arguably the most visible expression of Christian orphan care today.

Here's how the *Wall Street Journal* described it in 2010: "As more and more evangelical churches take up the cause of adoption on a large scale, their congregations have begun to look like the multiracial sea of faces that Christian leaders often talk about wanting."[24] According to our FRAMES research, nearly one-third of churches today actively encourage attendees to consider foster care and adoption.

Children need families to thrive. Yet millions today face the world without one. For children who lack parents, adoption into a caring family means the lifelong love, protection, and nurture every child deserves.

Most children available for adoption today—both in the United States and internationally—are not healthy infants. This is in part due to politically motivated restrictions on international adoption, like Russia's recent ban on adoptions to the US. But it is also due

It's typically easiest to find homes for healthy and young babies, but many people—Christians in particular—feel called to adopt older children or kids with special needs.

AVERAGE AGE OF ORPHANS*

0-4: **15**%

5-9: **35**%

10-14: **50**%

49%

*of all foster children who were adopted in 2012 were under age 5***

*Source: UNICEF-MICS, 1997–2002 | **Source: AFCARS Report, July 2013

to the fact that only a small percentage of children are orphaned at birth. Those orphaned as babies are most likely to be adopted locally. If a baby is placed in an orphanage, it may be years before the child becomes officially eligible for international adoption. As a result, the majority of kids currently available for adoption are those who are older, have special needs, or are part of sibling groups.

Christians are increasingly embracing these more challenging situations, including adopting or fostering older children and sibling groups. Others are adopting children with special needs that range from medically repairable conditions like a cleft palate to lifelong challenges such as HIV, Down syndrome, and hearing and sight impairment. Bethany Christian Services, the nation's largest Christian adoption agency, reports that in 2012, 57% of all of its adoption placements were of children that came with special needs. When counting only inter-country adoptions, the percentage with special needs rises to approximately 80%.[25]

Global Orphan Care

Financially speaking, the lion's share of investment by Christians in caring for orphans worldwide flows into a vast array of in-country care programs. These efforts are highly diverse, often supported by both local and international funding, staff, and volunteers. They range from group homes and orphanages, to in-country adoption and foster initiatives, to programs that enable struggling orphan-widow families to stay together.

How willing would you be to adopt a child ...

WITH MENTAL SPECIAL NEEDS?

All adults

| 11% | 25% | 28% | 36% |

Practicing Christians

| 15% | 26% | 30% | 29% |

WITH PHYSICAL SPECIAL NEEDS?

All adults

| 11% | 28% | 27% | 35% |

Practicing Christians

| 13% | 30% | 29% | 28% |

OVER AGE 10?

All adults

| 17% | 34% | 21% | 28% |

Practicing Christians

| 21% | 34% | 20% | 26% |

WITH AN ADDICTION?

All adults

| 11% | 29% | 26% | 34% |

Practicing Christians

| 15% | 32% | 25% | 29% |

● Very　　● Somewhat　　● Not too　　● Not at all

GIVING TO THE ORPHAN

While charitable giving in general has increased, giving toward orphan care and adoption, in particular, has dramatically increased.

2011

Overall charitable giving:
up 4%

Christian donations to

Adoption: **up 12.4%**

Orphan care: **up 11.8%**

2012

Overall charitable giving:
up 3.5%

Christian donations to

Adoption: **up 10%**

Orphan care: **up 17%**

*Sources: USA Today and The Evangelical Council for Financial Accountability

Christian giving to a range of orphan-related causes has grown dramatically in recent years. Charitable giving by Americans in 2011 rose about 4%.[26] Giving to Christian orphan care rose by 11.8% and to adoption by 12.4%.[27] The most recent data reflect a continuation of this remarkable trend. All charitable giving in 2012 rose about 3.5%.[28] Giving by Christians to adoption rose by nearly 10% and to orphan care by more than 17%.[29]

We can celebrate this growing commitment to the good of orphans even while urging caution. As we'll explore later, if poorly planned and executed, even our best attempts to do good sometimes accomplish little. They may even do harm.

The best Christian orphan care efforts are relentless in their commitment to both biblical principles and best practice models. They also work hard to ensure that Western NGOs are not viewed as the sole answer to local ills. Rather, they aim always to ensure that whenever possible the *local church* stands at the center of solutions. Western organizations can play a vital role to empower local leaders. This approach can be slower and more complicated, but it ultimately nurtures solutions that impact longer and deeper than those imported from afar.

(Visit www.cafo.org/becominghome for "Core Principles" affirmed by the Christian Alliance for Orphans and also for questions to ask orphan care organizations before investing in their work.)

Family Preservation

On an even broader level, it is important to recognize that the vast portion of dollars given by Christians to address human needs globally contributes to what many would consider "family preservation." The countless Christian health, micro-finance, disaster relief, community development, and related efforts prevent children from becoming orphans by helping hard-pressed families stay together. Although rarely billed as "orphan prevention" programs, they do just that.

One sees this commitment to elevating families from poverty almost everywhere Christians are serving — from the $2.79 billion budget of World Vision International[30] to the 1.4 million vulnerable children sponsored through Compassion International.[31]

Even many orphan-focused organizations contribute significantly to family preservation efforts.

The size of these programs often dwarfs those focused solely on caring for orphaned children. This is as it should be, since it is always far preferable to prevent a child from becoming an orphan in the first place. But these twin commitments—to family preservation and to more focused care for children who lack families—need not be seen as competitive. Rather, both are vital expressions of a commitment to orphans and widows in distress.

Often, these two involvements come together. For example, eleven Christian families who adopted from Ethiopia in recent years have banded together to raise funds for in-country orphan care and family preservation efforts in Ethiopia. In just over a year, they have raised more than $600,000 for facilities. They have also helped secure sponsors for more than four hundred children for ongoing schooling and basic nutrition, helping to preserve families who face the risk of disintegration due to financial strain.[32]

Foster Care

The growing commitment to children who lack the care of parents extends not only to the other side of the world; it also seeks out needs on the other side of town.

The US foster care system is not an easy place to be—whether as a child, a foster parent, a birthparent who has had their child removed from their home, or a social worker. Like any government system, it can be harsh and illogical at times.

Families who provide foster care sometimes find that dealing with the system itself can be the most taxing aspect. That's a big reason nearly half of foster parents quit within a year of their first placement.[33] It is also a reminder that no one family should have to walk the road of foster care alone. It's a vision for a church community to take on together.

One sees this vibrantly in Colorado, where many churches have made kids in the foster system a central focus. Over the past four years, the number of children waiting to be adopted in Colorado has been cut from 677 to less than 300.[34] Dr. Sharen Ford, who oversees foster care adoptions for the state, said, "There is no question who is doing it. It's the

FOSTERING BY THE NUMBERS
in 2012

399,546
*children in foster care
in the US*

101,719
*foster kids eligible
for adoption*

7.8
*average age of
foster child waiting
to be adopted*

52,039
*kids adopted from
foster care*

23,439
*kids who 'aged out'
of the foster system*

*Source: AFCARS Report, July 2013

church families adopting these precious children that no one else would take in the past."[35]

Similar efforts are springing up across the country, from California to Kentucky, to Texas to Washington, DC.[36] In Broward County, Florida, most every child who enters the region's massive foster system is touched at least once by the network of churches led by 4KIDS of South Florida—from the 4KIDS assessment center to foster care, independent living, support for girls with an unplanned pregnancy, mentoring, and adoption.[37]

It is essential to remember that in most foster situations, the hope is that the child will be able to reunite safely with his or her family of birth. That often isn't possible, and the parental rights of nearly 60,000 US children were terminated in 2012 alone. But Christians who open themselves to foster care need to understand that the healing of entire families is—and must be—the highest goal whenever possible.

One cutting-edge Christian program works to prevent

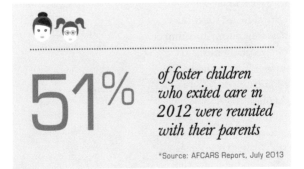

51%

of foster children who exited care in 2012 were reunited with their parents

*Source: AFCARS Report, July 2013

children from entering foster care in the first place. "Safe Families," pioneered by Dr. David Anderson in Illinois, works with the state to provide an all-volunteer alternative to the foster system. Children temporarily cared for by Safe Families volunteer host families are not entangled in the legal system as they would be with foster care. As a result, children are able to reunite more readily with their birthparents, many of whom receive support through Safe Families. Last year alone, more than 900 children in the Chicago region were cared for in Christian homes at no cost to the state. State officials informally estimate the program has saved taxpayers more than $30 million. Today, the Safe Families model is being replicated in sixty-five sites across the United States and also in the United Kingdom.[38]

FOSTER KIDS
who are eligible for adoption

.... 11%
.... 41%
.... 23%
.... 26%

FOSTER KIDS
who were adopted

.... 10%
.... 46%
.... 21%
.... 23%

● White   ● Hispanic
● Black   ● Other

*Source: AFCARS Report, July 2013

Support for Local Movements Worldwide

Increasingly, churches in developing countries are also embracing a vision for locally led adoption and orphan care efforts.

In Ethiopia, a group called Kidmia helps place orphans for adoption in local families. In Costa Rica, Casa Viva has pioneered a church-based foster care model. In China, Care for Children has transitioned more than 250,000 children from orphanages to homes. Lifesong for Orphans provides financial and other support for local adoptions in Eastern Europe. Saddleback Church has been working with the Rwandan government and churches to boost local adoptions.[39]

Often, these initiatives rise as true partnerships between the local and the global church. Western Christians may provide support, but it's the local believers who are leading. In some cases, such as with Ukraine Without Orphans, the impact is truly transforming how local Christians see orphans and act on their behalf. (See the RE/Frame from Ruslan Maliuta on what is happening in Ukraine on page 83).

The success of efforts like these offers glimpses of the ultimate goal: a day when the local church in every nation has become home for the orphans in its midst.[40]

Redemptive Hospitality

To care for wounded children requires more than individuals alone. Rather, foster care, adoption, and other ways of loving orphans call the entire church

community to embrace children together. It is a vision for *redemptive hospitality*, welcoming those who'd been unwelcomed and alone. It's about the family of God *becoming home* to those who ache for one.[41] This can be acted out in ways large and small.

When Rachel and I were adopting, several other families helped bear the financial costs with us. When Ayana died, friends from church organized a memorial service to enable the whole community to grieve with us. Later, when we brought our daughter Eden home, they gave gifts and celebrated with us. For more than a year, a retired friend did most of our grocery shopping.

Through my work with the Christian Alliance for Orphans, I hear similar stories from across the country. Young adults offer babysitting to give adoptive and foster parents a break.

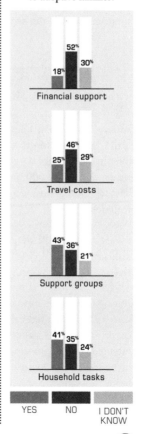

How Churches Help

Practicing Christians identify the following ways their churches are offering help to adoptive families:

Financial support
18% · 52% · 30%

Travel costs
25% · 46% · 29%

Support groups
43% · 36% · 21%

Household tasks
41% · 35% · 24%

YES | NO | I DON'T KNOW

Empty nesters run errands and help with yard care. A mechanic teaches foster youth simple car maintenance. Hairstylists offer free haircuts every other month. Others can just invite over for a BBQ "the extra large family" or "the family with special needs."

All these acts can make a world of difference practically. They also convey something even more valuable to both parent and child: *You are most welcome here.*

HAZARDS OF CARING IN A BROKEN WORLD

January 12, 2010, 4:53 p.m. For ninety seconds, the earth trembled. Homes—mostly of cement block and other brittle materials—crumbled as residents tried to escape. Some 280,000 buildings fell. Ultimately, more than 100,000 people were killed and vast numbers wounded.

A wide array of Christian ministries and other non-profits had been serving in Haiti for decades. They were soon joined by countless other groups.

Among the people moved to help was a band of ten Americans from a recently formed orphan ministry based in Idaho. Its leader, Laura Silsby, had previously intended to build an orphanage for Haitian children in the neighboring Dominican Republic. But following the earthquake, she and nine other volunteers landed in the Dominican Republic. They leased a forty-five-room hotel before forging across the border into Haiti on a rented bus. They aimed to gather one hundred orphans and bring them back to safety and care.

It was a vision spurred by compassion and a desire to do good. Yet it was begun with little planning or preparation. Neither Silsby nor the team possessed more than cursory knowledge of local culture and language or best practices in emergency relief. In the words of Proverbs, it was zeal without knowledge. The result, predictably, was disastrous.

After rounding up thirty-three children in Haiti, the group headed back to the border. Although warned not to do so by both Christian missionaries and police in Haiti, Silsby tried to remove the children from Haiti without permission. She and the others were arrested and jailed on trafficking charges. It was soon discovered the thirty-three children were not double orphans as Silsby believed. In fact, every one of them had at least one living parent.

Good Intentions Aren't Enough

The point of a story like this is not to bash a well-meaning person like Laura Silsby and her group. I suspect God will find more to praise in those who stumble as they seek to do good than in those who do not act at all.

Nor is the point that Christians have the market cornered on defective attempts at compassion. Even as stories about Silsby's debacle filled headlines, UN peacekeepers inadvertently imported a virulent strain of cholera to Haiti—which ultimately took the lives of some eight thousand Haitians.[42] The history of philanthropy is riddled with good intentions gone awry, both religious and secular.

Our takeaway is simply this: Attempts to address deep human need are thick with hazards, so good intentions are not enough.

With that in mind, here are five of the most common dangers inherent in orphan care:

1. Underestimating the Challenge of Doing Orphan Care Well

These kids have no parents. How tough can it be to make their life better? I'll come in with some food first, clothes, camp, maybe get a big sports program going. Shouldn't be difficult to help.

It's hard not to feel this way, at least at first. But the closer we get to any deep human need, the more we see that every thread we pull is connected to countless others. One well-meant tug can create a tangle of knots in ways we'd never imagined.

This is true with all forms of orphan care. Importing shoes and bed nets can prevent disease, but it may also drive local providers of these goods out of business. Starting an orphanage may rescue many children from the streets, but soon children may choose to leave good homes for the orphanage with hopes of a decent education or adequate meals. Shifting kids from an orphanage to foster care may offer a more home-like setting for orphans, but it may also place children in danger of being exploited for labor or sex.

Of course, all of this complexity is no excuse for inaction. It simply reminds us that caring for orphans is not something to do halfway or on a whim. We must know that addressing serious needs—whether as professionals or volunteers—demands serious study, preparation, and planning.

For a list of key questions individuals and churches can ask of an international orphan care ministry before supporting their work, visit www.cafo.org/becominghome.

2. Underestimating the Ethical Hazards of International Adoption

International adoption carries great risk of unintended consequences. One of the biggest is the danger that the presence of US dollars could pull some children toward international adoption who'd be best served in other ways.

Certainly, funding is necessary to facilitate the costs of adoption. But these fees can climb higher than an average annual salary in some countries, so even good people can be tempted to move children toward adoption who might not really need it. For example, local "facilitators" in some countries have been known to actively recruit children for adoption, including some with intact families. Yes, claims that children are "kidnapped" or "trafficked" for adoption are often sensationalistic. But subtler forms of inappropriate adoption are a bigger risk.

Several years ago, the Bradshaw family in Iowa adopted three sisters from Ethiopia, believing their mother was dead and father was dying of AIDS. But once in Iowa, the girls reported to their new family that their father was well. He apparently gave his daughters for adoption with the double purpose of obtaining an education for them and a personal payment for himself.[43] In other cases, birthparents have been misled to believe adoption was only a temporary placement.

Situations like this represent a grave injustice. That's true whether they were caused by intentional deception or simply an end-justifies-the-means humanitarianism. Christians should be the most aggressive in seeking to guard against any such abuse.

Admittedly, working to prevent abuses can be a double-edged sword. To guarantee zero risk of errors in developing countries—or any country for that matter—would require shutting adoption systems entirely. At times, countries have done this, promising to re-open adoptions once systems can be considered problem-free. Predictably, that day often never comes.

Ultimately, we must know that no human system is without hazards. For example, a child dies in US foster care virtually every day of the year.[44] This fact is not "acceptable." Yet this imperfect system continues to be viewed as necessary. Why? Because error and unintended consequences will be a part of any undertaking, especially those that engage the world at its most broken. If our standard is perfection, we need to give up now — not only on adoption, but on every other effort to address human need.

Minimizing the potential for corruption and fraud in adoption is imperative. But constricting adoption rarely makes children safer. Often, it does just the opposite. Whether or not international adoption is allowed, children who lack parents continue to face the evils that especially threaten orphans, from disease to human trafficking. A permanent family — whether via local adoption or international adoption — presents the single greatest protection for the child who lacks parents.

Amidst these issues, one question may be the most complex of all: When should a birthparent be allowed to relinquish a child

HARD QUESTIONS

Parents and kids in the foster system face tough decisions, often with no clear-cut answers. Here's what Americans generally think when it comes to some of the tough fostering dilemmas.

49%
Say a child should be raised by whomever can provide the best home, even if it's not the biological parents

40%
Say a child should be removed from parents only if the child is in immediate danger

6%
Say a child should be removed if the parents have a hard time caring for them

5%
Say a child should be raised by biological parents, even if it's a rough home

for adoption? It's my belief that a child should never be accepted for adoption if financial need is the only reason for relinquishment.

Of course, when parents consider relinquishing a child, financial poverty is often intertwined with far deeper issues that may not be solvable: a pregnant teen who desires to continue her education without a child or a new stepfather who wants nothing to do with his wife's children. So determining what is truly best for a child is never easy. But Christian adoption agencies and families should be known as the most vigilant in seeking to prevent adoptions driven solely by poverty. When that appears to be the case, every effort should be made to both persuade and empower the parent to raise the child at home.

To help hold adoption agencies to the highest standards, see "12 Questions for Prospective Adoptive Parents to Ask of Adoption Agencies" at www.cafo.org/becominghome.

3. Thinking Too Big

When we desire to solve big problems, most of us tend to want to do it on a big scale. Large orphanages promise to do that—providing shelter, food, education, and more for dozens or even hundreds of children under one roof. These physical provisions can indeed help children survive. But what children need most to thrive goes much deeper.

Children need love, nurture, and belonging or they

will emotionally shrivel. This sticks us with a painful dilemma: Millions of children lack families, yet what they most need cannot be purchased and delivered in bulk. Each one requires loving, long-term relationship. This is a mass-scale problem that cannot be solved en masse. It must be addressed one precious child at a time.

Both Scripture and social science affirm that the very best environment for a child is a caring family. Children who grow up in orphanages without consistent, nurturing adult relationships rarely do well. Even when needs for food and shelter are met, such children are often stunted physically, emotionally, intellectually, and relationally. One startling yet representative study in Romania by Harvard professor Charles Nelson found that up to age three, children's IQ decreased by nearly one point for every two months spent in an orphanage.[45] Another meta-analysis reviewing seventy-five studies covering nineteen countries found that the average IQ of children living in orphanages was twenty points lower than those living in families.[46]

Dr. Nelson's study found that children placed in homes via foster care fared much better that those in institutions. Best of all were those placed in a permanent family while still young—quickly catching up to their non-orphaned peers.

We see this even with the relatively well-funded US foster system. The future awaiting young adults who grow up in the US foster system without being adopted is sheer tragedy. By their mid-twenties, less than half are employed. More than 60% of males have been incarcerated as adults versus 9% of men overall.[47] With

WITHOUT ADOPTION, A DISMAL FUTURE

At age 26 ...

● Foster youth who age out of care ● General population

High school education or less
60%
28%

4-year degree or more
4%
36%

Currently employed
46%
80%

Could not pay rent in last year
28%
6%

Women receiving food stamps
68%
7%

Men ever incarcerated
64%
9%

Median income
$8,950 $27,310

*Source: AFCARS Report, July 2013

women, 68% are on food stamps, compared to 7% overall.[48]

Whether in Africa or Asia or America, every child needs a permanent family. Even as we champion this goal, however, we must also know our world's brokenness does not always allow for the ideal. In many situations, local culture has not yet embraced adoption, and international adoption is closed. Also, the deep needs of some children may require a more therapeutic environment than most families can provide. In cases like these, well-run residential facilities, especially smaller ones, provide an alternative far preferable to life on the streets. We can honor and support these efforts, even as we press always as close to the ideal as possible.

This understanding gives us three "Ps" to prioritize:

First: Preservation of Families — The very best way to guarantee a family for vulnerable children is to ensure they do not lose their family in the first place. So whenever it is possible to keep together a struggling family or safely reunite those who have been separated, family preservation should be sought before any other solution.

Second: Placement into Families — Children need families. So when preservation or reunification of the original family is not an option, a child deserves a new permanent family as soon as it is feasible — locally if possible and via international adoption if not.

Third: Proximate Families — Even with a bedrock commitment to family, we can also affirm the need for other solutions when the ideal is not achievable. Any such alternative—from foster care to group homes—should be as permanent, nurturing, and close to family as is feasible for the situation.

4. Failing to Grasp the Complexity of the Adoption Journey

Christian advocates for adoption at times have been guilty of "adoption cheerleading." Hoping to help others embrace the blessing of adoption, we can highlight adoption's joys without equally presenting its challenges.

This can lead to all manner of ills. When families adopt without preparing for what might be required to heal a wounded child, it is a recipe for heartache. Adoption is not merely a process—of paperwork, financial costs, and long waiting. Adoption is most of all a lifelong journey—discovery, sacrifice, and experiencing together both pain and joy. Like any journey, it requires both strong preparation in advance and allies to help along the way.

This is true for all expressions of care for orphans, not just adoption. From foster care to mentoring to global programs, whenever we open our lives to a child who has known great hurt, we will taste some of that hurt too. Encouraging people to get involved without offering the full picture guarantees disillusionment. If we are to love others as God first loved us, we must embrace both its beauty and its costliness.

A number of wise Christian counselors and researchers provide excellent guidance on how to help wounded children heal. These include Dr. Karyn Purvis (*The Connected Child*), Jayne Schooler (*Wounded Children, Healing Homes*), Dr. Curt Thompson (*Anatomy of the Soul*), and Deborah Gray (*Attaching in Adoption*).

Finally, we must never forget that there is always a third figure in every adoption story, too often disregarded: the birthmother. She may be the victim of HIV in Malawi, or an executive in Manhattan, or in prison for drug use. But whatever the details, her story matters. She matters. And although it may be complex, those who care about adoption must care about each birthmother as well — both as an individual and as the one who gave her child the gift of life.

5. Assuming the Savior Complex

Any effort to help others can quickly become about us. We come to see ourselves as noble rescuers, riding into perilous situations on a white horse. Words we use can perpetuate this narrative, such as "rescuing orphans" and "saving children."

Of course, these words are not bad themselves. The world is full of children who do need rescue. But when our narrative subtly becomes "us as rescuers," we are in serious danger. What often follows is the pride, self-focus, and I-know-better outlook that have been at the root of countless misguided efforts to help others.

This can be especially corrosive in how we come to see

and speak of children themselves. Children are never a "cause." Each one is a person of matchless worth, utterly unique. They need to know they are embraced not as a "noble undertaking" but because someone is truly crazy about them. Whether as adoptive or foster parents or advocates for orphan care, both our language and our actions must keep this truth foremost.

Thankfully, Christians have no need to find our identity in being "the rescuer." *We* are the rescued. Even our best efforts are simply small, imperfect reflections of the way we have first been loved. This truth frees us from the compulsion to charge out to solve the world's problems alone. Rather, we are released to begin by listening and learning—from those who've gone before and from those we desire to serve. If we start here, we will rarely go wrong.

Choosing to Act Despite the Dangers

Anyone who dares to engage the world at its most hurting must know this: The results of even our best efforts will often be much less than we'd hope. We'll likely be disappointed by those we seek to serve—and they will be disappointed by us too. At countless crossroads along the way, we will face vexing dilemmas to which there are no good answers. To act at all, we'll have to choose among imperfect options that threaten heartbreaking side effects. From risks of corruption in adoption processes to abusive foster homes, we'll ache at unintended consequences.

Even a glimpse of all this complexity can be paralyzing.

Like the risk-averse investor in Jesus' parable of the talents, we may be tempted to bury what we have to offer and not get involved at all. But Jesus minced no words in condemning that approach. He called it "wicked and lazy." Instead, God calls us to act despite the risks. Understanding that helping can hurt gives us much-needed caution and humility. So we begin with learning, listening, planning, and only then, finally, action—always ready to recalibrate when we discover the mistakes we'll inevitably make.

Here, in humility and listening, is where a truly transformative journey begins.

LOVE FOR ORPHANS TRANSFORMS

Esther was nine when her father left. In some ways, it was a relief. He'd been highly unstable, often abusive. Her mom remarried when Esther reached sixth grade. But the second guy was no better than the first. Esther felt little when he walked out on them after just two years.

Esther heard soaring words about God in churches. They often rang hollow. Her heart yearned to know a good God. But if this heavenly Father was anything like what she'd experienced of earthly fathers, she'd be better off without him.

Little in Esther's experience was consistent except disappointment. She attempted suicide. Then Esther's mother—shattered by life—finally turned on her too. She locked the door on Esther and told her not to come back. For a teen without a family, the outcome was inevitable: foster care, or maybe a group home with other wounded girls.

But word about Esther's predicament spread among friends and acquaintances at a local church, the closest thing to family she'd known. Several helped in various ways: meals, clothes, a temporary guest room. And then, before the county could place her in the system, she got an invitation. It was from Luther and Rebecca Elliss, a couple in the church who already had a brood of both adopted and biological children. "If you want, we'd all love for you to come live with us, Esther," they offered. "You can stay as long as you want."

So she did. For the first time, Esther came home to a place defined by welcome and grace, not tumult. She experienced both firm boundaries and consistent love. She observed it was possible for a man to be both strong—Luther is six feet eight and nearly 325 pounds of muscle—and tender. She saw that a husband and wife could treat each other with honor, even in conflict.

"It utterly changed the trajectory of my life," Esther said. Less than 4% of former foster youth get a four-year degree by their mid-twenties, but Esther did.[49] And all throughout college, the home she returned to was the Ellisses'. It still is, more than a decade later. "You never outgrow a need for family," she explained. "And when I get married someday, Luther is the one I want walking me down the aisle."

Best of all, Esther now radiates the same love as the Ellisses. She's also served as a public advocate for committed marriage and faith-rooted family, to great effect. After all, Esther knows as well as any what a difference they can make.

Changing Children, Families, Churches, and the World Beyond

Here we come to the most beautiful truth of all: Love for orphans transforms.

It Transforms Children

Both anecdotes and data prove beyond doubt: Love and belonging change the trajectory of a child's life, from foster care to support of widow-and-orphan families. This transformation is vivid in adoptive families too. Despite the special challenges that can come with adoption, research consistently shows that adopted children thrive in loving homes. An expansive 1994 study by the Search Institute comparing adopted teens to other teens found:[50]

- Adopted teens scored higher on indicators of well-being such as school performance, friendships, volunteerism, self-esteem, and optimism.

- Adopted teens scored lower on indicators of high-risk behavior such as depression, alcohol use, vandalism, and police trouble.

- Children adopted trans-racially showed no differences in terms of identity formation and self-esteem, attachment to parents, or psychological health.

Findings like these are especially significant when one considers the heartrending outcomes for children who grow up without permanent families. Even when children adopted from difficult backgrounds struggle, studies show they fare far better than orphaned peers who were never adopted.

It Transforms Individuals and Families

Love for orphans changes the lives of children, to be sure. But that's not all. As a friend who helps churches in Arkansas get involved with foster care described, "I see the children changed. I see those families changed even more." As we encounter Jesus in the destitute child, Christians are pulled beyond a flaccid, self-focused religion to a costly-but-muscular faith.

I think of Roger in Southern California. He shared with me how his once-vibrant faith had grown cynical and uninspired. He formerly led a significant youth ministry; now even the thought of attending church left him dry. But through some friends, Roger and his wife had begun providing for the education and shelter of an orphaned girl in Haiti. As he did, Roger began to ponder the fact that God's concern for that girl was every bit as strong as for his own children, who were so well cared for and loved. When a hurricane destroyed the orphan home the girl lived in, Roger and some friends held a fundraiser to rebuild it.

And he keeps getting pulled deeper. Roger now finds himself in Haiti several times a year as part of an ongoing ministry to orphans. He told, "I don't know exactly what's happening here. All I know is that when my friends and I used to get together, all we'd talk about is surfing. Now we talk about caring for orphans. I think I'm beginning to rediscover my own faith as well."

It Transforms Churches

Love for orphans transforms churches as well. It helps us to see God's true character more than any sermon. As we support each other amid the joys and struggles of loving children from difficult places, we are knit ever closer as community.

In Costa Rica, Pastor Arturo Barrientes led his church to begin caring for orphans through a local foster care program. He and his wife set the example, welcoming a little girl named Brittany for two years. Many other families in the church are now doing the same.

Arturo believes they are on a journey that has just begun. But already he feels something significant has changed in the church. The depth of need in the city around them—always visible, but sometimes forgotten—has become much more real. Arturo's face lights up when he describes how the church has rallied to support fostering families in prayer, financially, with clothes, by babysitting, and more. It has "brought us together as a team," he says.

Arturo notes that the church had always supported many good ministries. "But with these children coming into our church," he continues, "we have deepened our understanding of what Christianity is really about."

Arturo concludes, "All of this isn't ultimately about the challenges we go through to care for the children. It has to do with grace. We all have been adopted. God's grace has come to our lives. What we are doing is just to give a little bit of what we have received. And what we understand is that when we give the grace we have received, it will be beautiful, but sometimes it will break your heart. I have never seen our church so broken than now—as we come to understand these children's stories and also see the impact that God's love can have on them through us."

It Transforms a Watching World

Finally, love for orphans transforms a watching world, as it sees—perhaps for the first time—the gospel embodied.

Another pastor friend, Daniel Bennett, helped his church in Peoria, Illinois, start a foster and adoption ministry. He saw it not only as a "justice ministry" but also as a venture of both discipleship and evangelism.

He's seen that hope validated again and again. Daniel describes what is happening now: "As our church grows excited about orphan ministry, I see people coming to grasp the love of God more deeply. I also see it growing our understanding of biblical love—that it involves real

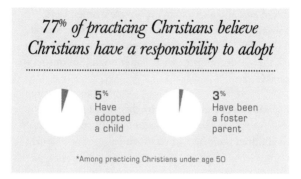

77% of practicing Christians believe Christians have a responsibility to adopt

5%
Have adopted a child

3%
Have been a foster parent

*Among practicing Christians under age 50

sacrifice; it gives like God does to those who have no way to pay you back."

This counter-cultural hospitality for hurting children reverberates beyond the church. Daniel goes on: "People outside our church who you never would have expected are intrigued, asking questions, because they're seeing the adoptions and care for the foster kids. It really gives the church a more powerful testimony to the community."

That is how the church has always been known at its best. Around AD 200, the apologist Tertullian wrote, "It is our care for the helpless, our practice of loving kindness, that brands us in the eyes of many of our opponents."[51]

Increasingly, the same can be said today. In Portland — the third "least religious" metro area in America — the *Oregonian* recently reported on what it called "a revolution in Portland's foster care." Dozens of area churches have joined together to serve kids in the foster system and also the system's oft-overwhelmed staff. A twenty-year veteran of the child welfare system said of the effort, "It's everything to say we're all in this together ... I cannot express that enough. I'm moved to tears. Often."[52]

Imagine the church defined by this — not primarily by what we oppose, but by a rare and profligate hospitality for children the world often discards.

BECOMING HOME

When Esther reflects on the life she's had since the Ellisses brought her into their family, she is quick to say the transformation runs deeper than the shelter, calm, and good food of a welcoming home. The source runs deeper even than kindness and belonging. She puts it like this: "All my life I'd heard about God's love and God as my father. But I don't think I ever really believed it 'til I experienced it through the Ellisses."

It is not only the fatherless who need to experience this. We all do. The question that lurks in the darkest recesses of the human heart is not whether God exists. Despite our doubts, most of us know deep down that he does. What we most question — what we really yearn to know — is whether he truly is the loving Father some people claim.

Coming to grasp God's heart for the fatherless begins to change that. When we hear from Scripture that God is especially tender and near to the destitute child, we start to hope he might be willing to come near to us too. For we too are those destitute children. And when we see God's love for orphans reflected by his people in real, tangible ways, we begin to be able to believe it all might be true. Because whenever and wherever Christians become home for the orphan, they point ultimately to an even greater reality. They remind that at the center of all things is the Father who pursued us at immeasurable cost to himself—who now welcomes us home as his daughters and sons.

EPILOGUE

Dorothy was born, married, and grew to middle age in the Ugandan village of Bundibugyo. But in 2001, the Congolese army crossed the nearby border and ravaged the village. Those who survived the attack struggled through the next two years in a refugee camp. Many died, including Dorothy's husband.

When Dorothy finally returned to Bundibugyo, she was unable to claim her home. She eked out a meager existence with odd jobs and the charity of neighbors. When she heard her pastor teaching that God had entrusted everyone with a gift to manage for his kingdom, Dorothy found it hard to agree. She had no home or income. God had not trusted her with anything, Dorothy concluded. She had nothing to offer.

But then one day it struck her. Yes, God had given her something! Dorothy entered church that Sunday with her heart full. Her words spilled out to the congregation, reminding them that 126 children in Bundibugyo had been orphaned by the war and disease.

She declared, "God has trusted me with the heart of a mother, and if you will trust me with one of these orphans, I will raise it as my own."

Many in the room that day felt not only admiration for Dorothy's faith but also deeply convicted. If an impoverished widow can do that, could not we too? One by one, families began to follow Dorothy's example. Within two months, one hundred families adopted all 126 orphans. Other families played a vital role also, aiding adoptive families with extra food, school fees, household help, and other support. Acting together, the church community ensured that not one child would grow up on the streets or in an orphanage. Each has a family to call its own.[53]

When it comes to caring for orphans, every believer has something to give. So you might ask, what about me? With what has God entrusted me? Where can I begin? I'd encourage you to start with three simple choices:

Prayer: Pray for the needs of orphaned children both near and far. Pray that Christians would rise as the answer for each child's need. As you do, ask God what role he may have for you in that.

Conversation: Talk with those who've gone before — in adoption, foster care, and/or global engagement. Each story is unique, so talk to many. Seek a deeper grasp of the real needs ... and the joys and challenges of getting involved.

One Small Step: Choose one action and do it, even if it's very simple. Attend an introductory class on foster care, volunteer to help a fundraiser, ask your pastor if you can lead a Sunday morning prayer for orphans, or take a social worker to lunch. Often, God will turn a small step of faith into an unforgettable journey. (See www.cafo/becominghome for ideas — "12 Ways to Love the Orphan.")

What might it look like if you chose to become home for a child who needs it?

What if your church became home for many?

What if all churches were known especially for that — as home for those who desperately need it?

What if just one in every three churches in America adopted a single child from foster care — reducing the number of children in America waiting for families to essentially zero?

What if churches across the world followed the example of Dorothy and her church community in Bundibugyo?

We've seen glimpses of what is possible throughout this book. To be sure, love for orphans comes with the loss of things the world most values: comfort, convenience, and control. But whatever the details, your story would almost certainly be one filled with beauty and heartache, joy and sorrow, struggle and celebration, painful missteps and wondrous things only God could bring about.

What could be better than that? ◆

BECOMING HOME

Adoption, Foster Care, and Mentoring—Living Out
God's Heart for Orphans

RE/FRAME

BY FRANCIS CHAN, CARISSA WOODWYK,
RUSLAN MALIUTA, DAVID PLATT, AND JIM DALY

When Christians care for orphans, it's not about us being rescuers. It's about understanding something far deeper: Jesus rescued me! You and I, we are children of God! We can celebrate that we are no longer orphans. We are loved by this Father — the One who calls himself Father to the fatherless, protector, defender, provider. That is at the core of God's stance for the hurting and vulnerable. We are in his eternal family.

This overflow of joy is what makes us desire to protect and care for children in need. We want to do a little bit of what God did for us. When we do, we don't just preach the gospel — we embody it. We give a picture of the fact that we have been adopted by God and that he takes us on as his children.

We can tell people about God the Father, and they may or may not listen. But when we represent God by what we do, by taking kids into our own homes, by loving them, by supporting others who adopt, others will notice.

Adoption, foster care, or any other practical way we defend the fatherless — all these things reflect God's character. It's an unforgettable portrait of what God did first for each of us. And when we love the fatherless, we come face-to-face with this incredible love, again and again, day after day. ◆

....

Francis Chan is the author of *Crazy Love*. For video of Francis sharing about what it means to love orphans, visit www.cafor .org/becominghome.

Orphans are often labeled as voiceless, vulnerable, helpless, forgotten. But let me tell you something. We adoptees, we're just like you—worthy, lovable, capable.

Like you, we have a story to tell, a voice to offer. We're learning to trust, and we are being healed. We have hope. We don't need you to rescue us; we need you to see us—the beautiful parts and the broken parts alike. We need you to remind us of who we are, who we were created to be.

All that to say, we want you to listen.

What does that really look like? How do you hear what's really being said behind the voice, behind the eyes, behind the behavior? How do you begin hearing those who hold a wound so deep it was delivered before they can even remember—a wound that continues to ache today with the longing to feel significant, wanted, loved?

We want you to listen to our hearts—our loss, our heartache, our journey, our restoration. To listen without assumption. And then to respond.

No, you don't *have* to. But you get to. And there's something here for all of us.

You, me, us, them—we get to be in this together. As you forge relationships with us, you get to model vulnerability and cultivate courage and build trust and offer grace. You get to show a real-life, real-time picture of Jesus and his heart for the orphan, for the world. And then, as that relationship becomes a two-way street, a sacred space is created. This is where healing can happen. And not just for us adoptees. This is where transformation can take place for us all.

But first, we need you to lean in, be still, be present, and listen. In the end, it just might change us all. ◆

....

Carissa Woodwyk was adopted as a child and is now an author and speaker. For video of Carissa sharing about learning to listen to the heart of an adoptee, visit www.cafor .org/becominghome.

Imagine a nation in which every child—every single child—had a place and a family to call home.

In 2009, that's what a group of Ukrainian Christian leaders came together to pray for and begin working toward. We began to imagine a Ukraine without orphans.

And over the years since, we've begun to see it happen. Adoption used to be a cultural oddity in my country, but today, churches and individuals are opening their hearts and homes to the orphans of Ukraine, even HIV-positive kids who need homes.

Not only are these children being elevated from a life of hopelessness, they are becoming agents of change themselves. Take, for example, the twenty adopted orphans who committed to riding around the world on their bikes. Crazy? Maybe. But if you ask them why, like a journalist asked one rider, it makes more sense. His answer? "I used to be an orphan, but now I have a father and a mother. My dream is for every orphan to experience the same, to see a world without orphans." The group covered more than six thousand miles over three years, telling their stories of adoption along the way.

These young adults are not the only ones whose lives are being changed. The Ukrainian church—across the spectrum from Protestant, Orthodox, and Catholic—is getting caught up in this movement of love for the orphan.

At a 2012 meeting of leaders of nineteen major Christian confessions, the chairman, who was at that time the head of the Catholic Church of Ukraine, said, "It's the first time in eighteen years of us meeting together that we are talking about orphans and what we can do to help them." Just a couple of months later, thousands of Christian congregations across the country celebrated Orphan Sunday.

Only a year later, UNICEF recognized Ukraine as the nation showing the most progress in child protection and welfare reform in Eastern Europe. Even the president of Ukraine caught our vision and is setting his goal for 2020 as the year no more children will live in institutions.

When you worship the God who loves the orphan and the widow, he will bring his vision about. He will place the lonely in families. ◆

....

Ruslan Maliuta is the founder of the Alliance for Ukraine Without Orphans. For video of Ruslan and other international leaders sharing about growing vision for orphan care and adoption in their countries, visit www.cafor.org/becominghome.

From cover to cover in Scripture, God displays his love as a Father to the fatherless. It's amazing what happens when his people begin to reflect that same heart.

Adoption, foster care, mentoring—these things are not easy. Challenges and even crises aren't uncommon. But one thing has become very clear: God's church is uniquely equipped for orphan care. Built into the community of faith is such an abundance of resources, people, and a wealth of love that stands ready to give to children who need families.

I love visiting our children's ministry programs at our church on a Sunday morning and seeing all the children who've been adopted and fostered. What's more, I see the whole church family loving, teaching, and raising these children and supporting their families.

In fact, it's brought us into understanding the heart of God and the gospel itself like never before. God is revealing to us—and to me personally as an adoptive father—more of himself. He's showing us vividly his pursuit of us as his children and his love for us as our Father. We find ourselves growing in our relationship with Christ, and growing in our love for one another and need for one another—all of this happening as we care for what God cares about. ◆

David Platt is the author of *Radical* and pastor of The Church at Brook Hills. For video of David sharing about how embracing a vision for foster care and adoption has impacted the church he pastors, visit www.cafor.org/becominghome.

"I never knew anything that good would come out of *Focus on the Family*." These words were spoken to me over coffee by John Weiss, the owner and publisher of the *Colorado Springs Independent*. For many years, the *Indy* has either ignored *Focus on the Family* or criticized it outright for its conservative approach to social issues.

But after stepping into the role of president at *Focus*, I began meeting with John on occasion for coffee. The more I learned of him, the more I respected his heart for our city. And during our conversations, he learned, for the first time, of our efforts to place orphans in loving families.

It was then that John made this admission. "For seventeen years," he said, "we've been carpet bombing you. We're going to wipe the slate clean."

And together, we did. Although we found ourselves on opposite sides of many issues, we discovered common ground in our shared passion for placing foster kids in forever families. So together, we planned an event to raise community awareness of the over three hundred local kids waiting to be placed with permanent families.

And with so many children still in need of families, we'll continue to work together and find common ground. ◆

....

Jim Daly is the president of *Focus on the Family* and was adopted as a child. For video of Jim sharing some of his own story as a child without parents, visit www.cafo.org/becominghome.

AFTER YOU READ

- Which story from the book most resonated with you?

- Why do you think it's so important to emphasize that orphan care comes out of the gospel story—out of God's adoption of lost, hurting people?

- Whom do you know who is caring for orphans? What are some needs you know they have? How can you find ways to serve them?

- Have you ever felt paralyzed by the fear of doing more harm than good? What are some practical ways you could address those fears and begin taking steps to help—while still being mindful of the potential dangers?

- What children in your community fit the biblical understanding of orphan—lacking the provision, protection, and nurture parents should provide? How could you and your church begin to think about ways of caring for these children?

- What is it about orphan care that you think transforms everyone? Why is this particular mandate such a central one for Christians?

- Orphan care is an issue that will tug at the heartstrings for most of us, but what do you feel God is asking *you* to do next?

SHARE THIS FRAME

Who else needs to know about this trend?
Here are some tools to engage with others.

SHARE THE BOOK

- Any one of your friends can sample a FRAME for FREE.
  Visit zondervan.com/ShareFrames to learn how.

- Know a ministry, church, or small group that would benefit
  from reading this FRAME? Contact your favorite bookseller, or
  visit Zondervan.com/buyframes for bulk purchasing information.

SHARE THE VIDEOS

- See videos for all 9 FRAMES on barnaframes.com and use
  the share links to post them on your social networks and share
  them with friends.

SHARE ON FACEBOOK

- Like facebook.com/barnaframes and be the first to see new
  videos, discounts, and updates from the Barna FRAMES team.

SHARE ON TWITTER

- Start following @barnaframes and stay current with the
  trends that are influencing and changing our culture.

- Join the conversation and include #barnaframes whenever
  you post a FRAMES related idea or culture-shaping trend.

SHARE ON INSTAGRAM

- Follow instagram.com/barnaframes for sharable visual
  posts and infographics that will keep you in the know.

Barna Group

 ZONDERVAN®

ABOUT THE RESEARCH

FRAMES started with the idea that people need simple, clear ideas to live more meaningful lives in the midst of increasingly complex times. To help make sense of culture, each FRAME includes major public-opinion studies conducted by Barna Group.

If you're into the details, the research behind the *Becoming Home* FRAME included 1,000 surveys conducted among a representative sample of adults over the age of eighteen living in the United States and its territories. This survey was conducted from July 29, 2013, through August 1, 2013. Additionally, 1,005 phone interviews were conducted from June 25, 2013, through June 29, 2013, with a 96% incidence rate and a 79% cooperation rate. The sampling error for both surveys is plus or minus 3 percentage points, at the 95% confidence level.

If you're really into the research details, find more at www.barnaframes.com.

ABOUT BARNA GROUP

In its thirty-year history, Barna Group has conducted more than one million interviews over the course of hundreds of studies and has become a go-to source for insights about faith and culture. Currently led by David Kinnaman, Barna Group's vision is to provide people with credible knowledge and clear thinking, enabling them to navigate a complex and changing culture. The company was started by George and Nancy Barna in 1984.

Barna Group has worked with thousands of businesses, nonprofit organizations, and churches across the country, including many Protestant and Catholic congregations and denominations. Some of its clients have included the American Bible Society, CARE, Compassion, Easter Seals, Habitat for Humanity, NBC Universal, the Salvation Army, Walden Media, the ONE Campaign, SONY, Thrivent, US AID, and World Vision.

The firm's studies are frequently used in sermons and talks. And its public-opinion research is often quoted in major media outlets, such as *CNN*, *USA Today*, the *Wall Street Journal*, Fox News, *Chicago Tribune*, the *Huffington Post*, the *New York Times*, *Dallas Morning News*, and the *Los Angeles Times*.

Learn more about Barna Group at www.barna.org.

THANKS

Even small books take enormous effort.

First, thanks go to Jedd Medefind for his passionate and compelling work on this FRAME — offering his experiences, both personal and professional, to create what we pray is a prophetic and challenging look at the call for all Christians to care for the orphan.

We are also incredibly grateful for the heartfelt contributions of Francis Chan, Carissa Woodwyk, Ruslan Maliuta, David Platt, and Jim Daly.

Next, Barna Group gratefully acknowledges the efforts of the team at HarperCollins Christian Publishing, especially Chip Brown and Melinda Bouma for catching the vision from the get-go. Others at HarperCollins who have made huge contributions include Jennifer Keller, Kate Mulvaney, Mark Sheeres, and Shari Vanden Berg.

The FRAMES team at Barna Group consists of Elaina Buffon, Bill Denzel, Traci Hochmuth, Pam Jacob, Clint Jenkin, Robert Jewe, David Kinnaman, Jill Kinnaman, Elaine Klautzsch, Stephanie Smith, and Roxanne Stone. Bill and Stephanie consistently made magic out of thin air. Clint and Traci brought the research to life — along with thoughtful analysis from Ken Chitwood. And Roxanne deserves massive credit as a shaping force on

FRAMES. Amy Duty did heroic work on FRAMES designs, from cover to infographics.

Finally, others who have had a huge role in bringing FRAMES to life include Brad Abare, Justin Bell, Jean Bloom, Patrick Dodd, Grant England, Esther Fedorkevich, Josh Franer, Jane Haradine, Aly Hawkins, Kelly Hughes, Steve McBeth, Geof Morin, Jesse Oxford, Beth Shagene, and Santino Stoner.

Many thanks!

NOTES

....

1. United Nations, "Child Adoption: Trends and Policies" (New York, United Nations, 2009), 17, http://www.un.org/esa/population/publications/adoption2010/child_adoption.pdf.

2. US Department of Health and Human Services, "National Survey of Adoptive Parents" (2007), 4.

3. US Department of Health and Human Services, Administration for Children and Families, "Trends in Foster Care and Adoption" (July 19, 2013), 1.

4. Widow's quote from UNICEF publication "Africa's Orphaned Generations," originally appeared in Erick Otieno Nyambedha, Simiyu Wandibba, and Jens Aagaard-Hansen, "Changing patterns of orphan care due to the HIV epidemic in western Kenya," *Social Science & Medicine*, 57, no. 2, July 2003, 301–11.

5. UNICEF, "Children and AIDS: Fifth Stocktaking Report, 2010," UNICEF, UNAIDS, WHO, UNFPA, and UNESCO, November 2010. This 2010 report estimates the total number of orphans at 153 million, with 17.8 million double orphans. A more recent report by UNICEF, "The State of the World's Children," reported an updated number of 151 million for all orphans (both single and double) but provides no number for double orphan estimates.

6. See, for example, Martha Ainsworth and Innocent Semali, "The Impact of Adult Deaths on Children's Health in Northwestern Tanzania, Volume 1," Policy Research Working Paper No. WPS 2266 (Washington, DC: World Bank, 2000). Or K. A. Lindblade, et al., "Health and nutritional status of orphans <6 years old cared for by relatives in western Kenya," *Tropical Medicine and International Health*, vol. 8, no. 1, January 2003, 67–72. Or the National Nutrition and EPI Survey, Ministry of Health and Child Welfare, Harare, Zimbabwe, 2003.

7. See, for example, Anne Case, Christina Paxson, and Joseph Ableidinger, "Orphans in Africa," Center for Health and Wellbeing and The Research Program in Development Studies, Princeton University, August 2002, http://www.princeton.edu/rpds/papers/pdfs/case_paxson_orphans_africa_press.pdf. Or Karin A. L. Hyde, et al., "HIV/AIDS and Education in

Uganda: Window of opportunity?" Rockefeller Foundation, January 2002, http://hivaidsclearinghouse.unesco.org/search/resources/1131_641Uganda HYDE.pdf.

8. Abiy Kifle, "Ethiopia—Child Domestic Workers in Addis Ababa: A Rapid Assessment" (Geneva: International Labour Organization, International Programme on the Elimination of Child Labour, July 2002).

9. "Rebuilding a life: A young girl struggles to overcome the trauma of trafficking," UNICEF, May 25, 2012, http://www.unicef.org/infoby country/moldova_24121.html.

10. A. C. S. Mushingeh, et al., "HIV/AIDS and Child Labour in Zambia: A rapid assessment on the case of the Lusaka, Copperbelt and Eastern Provinces," Paper No. 5 (Geneva/Lusaka: International Labour Organization, International Programme on the Elimination of Child Labour, August 2002).

11. Jessica Vander Velde, "FBI agent leads task force targeting pimps in child prostitution," *Tampa Bay Times*, July 30, 2013.

12. Cassi Feldman, "Report Finds 2,000 of State's Children Are Sexually Exploited, Many in New York City," *New York Times*, April 24, 2007.

13. "2013 AFCARS report #20," US Department of Health and Human Services, Children's Bureau.

14. See more at www.thepermanenceproject.org.

15. See more at " 'World without orphans' bicycle tour begins in Kiev," http://republicpilgrim.org/en/news/you-will-be-found/944.html.

16. See more at http://www.christianalliancefororphans.org/2011/06/28/earthy-expertise-and-kingdom-goals/.

17. Deuteronomy 10:18.

18. Hosea 14:3.

19. Psalm 68:5–6.

20. See, for example, 1 John 3:1 and Romans 9:26.

21. Learn more at www.bothhandsfoundation.org.

22. Alvin J. Schmitt, *How Christianity Changed the World* (Grand Rapids, MI: Zondervan, 2001), 53.

23. This quote came from a source document of *Didascalia Apostolorum*, known as *Testamentum Domini Nostri Jesu Christi*, ed. Arthur Voobus, The Synodicon in the West Syrian Tradition, CSCO 367 and 368, Scriptores Syri 161 and 162 (Louvain: Secretariat du CorpusSCO, 1975), 12 (Syriac), 35 English).

24. Naomi Riley, "Adoption Season for Evangelicals," *Wall Street Journal*, September 24, 2010.

25. Email to author from Kris Faase, Director of Adoption Services for Bethany Christian Services, confirmed on October 11, 2013.

26. Elizabeth Weise, "Charitable giving increased slightly in 2011," *USA Today*, November 27, 2012, http://www.usatoday.com/story/news/nation/2012/11/26/charitable-giving-increased-slightly/1728027/.

27. "2012 ECFA Annual State of Giving Report," Evangelical Council for Financial Accountability, December 14, 2012, http://www.ecfa.org/Content/2012-ECFA-Annual-State-of-Giving-Report.

28. Molly Vorwerck, "Charitable giving has slow, steady growth in 2012," *USA Today*, June 17, 2013, http://www.usatoday.com/story/news/nation/2013/06/17/charitable-giving-slow-2012/2432125/.

29. "2013 ECFA Annual State of Giving Report," Evangelical Council for Financial Accountability, unpublished as of the writing of this book, but confirmed via email with ECFA President Dan Busby.

30. "World Vision International Accountability Report 2011."

31. Compassion International, http://www.compassion.com/news-releases/compassion-international-appoints-new-president-ceo-jim-mellado.htm.

32. Ziway and Adami Tulu Project, http://www.ZATproject.com.

33. "Casey Foster Family Assessment Training Workbook," quoted by Jayne Schooler in "Why Are Foster Parents Leaving?," *Fostering Families Today*, September/October 2009, 23.

34. Electa Daper, "Adoption initiative halves numbers of kids needing families," *Denver Post*, March 5, 2010. Latest data is confirmed in email to author from Dr. Sharen Ford, Manager, Permanency Services, Colorado Department of Human Services.

35. Quote from author's conversation with Dr. Sharen Ford on November 12, 2012. Dr. Ford has articulated similar observations in a variety of public settings, including the 2012 Christian Alliance for Orphans' Summit.

36. DC127, http://www.dc127.org.

37. 4KIDS of South Florida, http://www.4kidsofsfl.org/. Details confirmed via email with 4KIDS Executive Director Tom Lukasik on July 23, 2013.

38. See more about Safe Families for Children, http://www.lydiahome.org.

39. See www.kidmia.com; www.lifesongfororphans.org; and www.casaviva.org.

40. See CATO Christian Alliance for Orphans, http://www.cafo.org/global

and also the exciting work of World Without Orphans, http://www
.worldwithoutorphans.org/.

41. Parts of this section are similar to an article I wrote for *Christianity Today*, which first appeared in the October 2013 edition.

42. Deborah Sontag, "In Haiti, Global Failures on a Cholera Epidemic," *New York Times*, March 31, 2012.

43. Armen Keteyian, "Child: U.S. Adoption Agency Bought Me," CBS News, February 16, 2010, http://www.cbsnews.com/stories/2010/02/15/cbsnews_investigates/main6210911.shtml.

44. See "2013 AFCARS report #20," page 3, which lists 328 deaths in foster care for FY 2012. This number has been significantly higher in prior years.

45. "Children Who Leave Orphanage Have Higher IQ," synopsis, Methods of Healing, http://www.methodsofhealing.com/children-who-leave-the-orphanages-have-a-higher-iq/.

46. Marinus H. van IJzendoorn, et al., "IQ of Children Growing Up in Children's Homes: A Meta-Analysis on IQ Delays in Orphanages," *Merrill-Palmer Quarterly* (Detroit: Wayne State University Press, July 2008), 341–66.

47. Mark E. Courtney, et al., "Midwest Evaluation of the Adult Functioning of Former Foster Youth: Outcomes at Age 26" (Chicago: University of Chicago, Chapin Hall, 2011), http://www.chapinhall.org/sites/default/files/Midwest%20Evaluation_Report_12_21_11_2.pdf.

48. Erik Eckholm, "Study Finds More Woes Following Foster Care," *New York Times*, April 7, 2010.

49. Courtney, "Former Foster Youth: Outcomes at Age 26," 21.

50. The Search Institute, "Growing Up Adopted" (Minneapolis, 1994).

51. This version of the quote drawn originally from James Moffatt's translation of Adolf Von Harnack's *The Expansion of Christianity in the First Three Centuries*, vol. 1 (New York: G. P. Putnam's Sons), 184. Other translations have slight variations on the original quote from *Tertullian's Apology*, section XXXIX.

52. Steve Duin, "A Revolution in Portland's Foster Care," *Oregonian*, May 20, 2013.

53. I heard this story from Bob Wielenga of International Steward. Learn more about the remarkable believers of Bundibugyo in "The Grace of Giving" video, http://internationalsteward.org/videos.